CW00403046

COUNTY DIALECT

A selection of words and anecdotes
from around County Durham

by
Hannah Pease

BRADWELL
BOOKS

Published by Bradwell Books
9 Orgreave Close Sheffield S13 9NP
Email: books@bradwellbooks.co.uk

All rights reserved. No part of this publication may be produced, stored in a retrieval system or transmitted in any form or by any means, electronic, mechanical, photocopying, recording or otherwise without the prior permission of Bradwell Books.

British Library Cataloguing in Publication Data: a catalogue record for this book is available from the British Library.

1st Edition

ISBN: 9781910551615

Typesetting by: Andrew Caffrey

Photograph Credits: iStock and selected images Reproduced by permission of Durham County Record Office. Images credited separately.

Print: Gomer Press, Llandysul, Ceredigion SA44 4JL

Introduction

If you really want to understand the history of a place, you need to get to know its dialect. Nowhere is this truer than for County Durham. Just a quick look at its dialect reveals the astonishing richness of its history. Whether it's Pitmatic, the language of the mining world, or its distinctive local phrases and sayings, the dialect of County Durham is packed full of its past. From the language once used by hard-working coal-hewers to the words and phrases on the lips of local people, we take a look at the language behind the place. With such a rich history of mining, it's no wonder that County Durham's history features not one, but two Pitman poets! In this book, we look at their contribution in celebrating the hardships and the humour involved with surviving everyday life in County Durham collieries.

There is so much to explore in the dialect and the history of County Durham that we could only cover a little in this book. Did you know that County Durham's miners loved to dance? Inside, we look at two types of dances which were once hugely popular in the area. We also explore the fascinating links between County Durham and Charles Dickens, Elizabeth Barrett Browning, English mustard and one half of one of the world's best-loved comic partnerships! Plus, we look at why the ancient story of a giant snake is so popular around the North-East. Read on to start discovering the dialect and history of County Durham for yourself!

Glossary

Animals and other creatures

Ask – a small lizard, or newt

Blackclock – cockroach

Cuddy – donkey

Dickyhedgie – hedge-sparrow

Galloway – pit pony

Jackjaw – jackdaw

Kitling – kitten

Loggerhead – a coloured butterfly. Large moths were also sometimes called loggerheads.

Peesweep – lapwing or peewit

Stonie – stallion

Home

Bedfast – bed-ridden

Cracket – a low stool, found in most cottages

Doorstead – threshold

Forenenst – facing opposite. Said about houses in a street.

Gulley – carving-knife, bread-knife. Also, a crevice.

Kist – chest of drawers

Longsettle – a long seat like a form, with back and arms

Recking-crook – a crook hanging over the fire for pans to hang from

Winter – the bracket which was hooked on to the bars of a grate, upon which anything could be heated in front of the fire

Yam – home. *'Aa's gannin yam, aa is.'*

Food and drink

Bullet – a type of sweet. A large sweetshop in one northern town bore the sign 'The Bullet King'.

Dough – cake. 'Yule-doo' was a kind of currant cake made in shape of a baby and given to children at Christmas.

Fine-tasted – fine-flavoured

Loppit – sour milk, curd milk

Paste-eggs (i e. Pasch-eggs) – eggs, dyed in a mix of logwood chips and onion peel, and sold in shops or prepared at home during Easter

Potted head – stewed meat, as sold in butchers' shops

Singing ninny – a kind of girdle-cake. Now generally called spice cake.

Spanish – liquorice

Spice – the only name known for currant cake. 'Cake' always referred to as tea-cake.

Toughcake – a water-cake, or white-cake, baked on a girdle. No currants were used.

Outdoors

Bank – hill. The word 'hill' was said to be almost unknown in the dialect. It was also the technical word for the 'pit'- surface, the top of the 'shaft'. 'To work at bank ' was to do the colliery work above ground.

Enter-common – a place open to everybody

Fad – farmyard

Fladges – snowflakes. Often called 'flatches'.

Garth – a potato field; also called 'Taty-garth'. More generally, a small enclosed grass field, near a home.

Ghyll – an area of wild ground hollowed out naturally; a ravine

Jumly – muddy

Outbye – out of the way, remote. Also the technical word for a miner coming towards the 'shaft' in order to get 'to bank'.

Pike – a large haycock, often six feet high. The small haycocks were called 'cocks'.

Stook – bundle of sheaves set up in the cornfield

People

Aud-farand – cunning, wise beyond your years

Callant – boy or girl

Fratchy or fratch – cross-tempered

Hempy – Up to tricks and pranks, mischievous. Also, hemp, a scamp.

A waterfall on the River Tees iStock

Pawky – dainty

Pittering – low-spirited, complaining

Sackless – foolish, senseless

Thropple – throat, windpipe

Twist – quarrel, disagreement

Unpatient – impatient

Outside G.E. Forster's cycle shop at 16 New Elvet, Durham, in the early 1900s Durham County Record Office D_CL0027_0277_0008

Leisure

Bowl – stone ball. The game was common in the North among pitmen. The one who threw the longest distance in three goes was declared the winner. The weight of the 'bowl' was 5oz, 15oz, 20oz and upwards.

Clish-clash – idle talk

Handball – the game of Bounders. More commonly called 'roondies'. Played by girls with shells ('williks') and a ball, while these words are recited:

Set a cup upon a rock,
Chalk me one a pot.
One, two, three, four,
One at a time, etc.
One up, etc.

Jolly Miller – a round game, with the words sung while playing:

There was a jolly miller, and he lived by himself,
As the mill went round he made his wealth;
One hand in the hopper [also 'copper'] and the other in the bag,
As the mill went round he made his grab [or 'brag'].

The players go two and two together, round and round, and there is always an odd one in the middle. When they come to the last word 'grab,' he makes a grab, forces another to come out, and takes his place; they then start again, singing as before.

Kenner – time to cease work

Library – a book from a library

Panker-bowdie – a game played with marbles. The 'panker' or 'penker' is a large marble, made of stone or iron. Each player would put four marbles in a ring, and proceed to knock them out of the ring with a 'panker'. What he knocked out he got; but if he failed to knock one out, the next boy aimed at his 'panker', and so put him out. The line from which they start, five yards from the ring, is called the 'bye'.

Shinny – hockey

Trippet and quoit – the game of Trap, Bat, and Ball, more commonly called 'Buck-stick'.

Work

Buzzer – the steam whistle or foghorn that warns miners of the times for returning to and from work

Checkweighman – the name for both the pit owner's and the people's representative, each appointed to check the other's honesty, in weighing coal-laden tubs, as they came from the pit

Chemmerly – urine kept in a large stone bottle and used for washing clothes

Face – the innermost part of the pit, where the hewers or stonemen are engaged at working into the solid coal

Longcart – a two-wheeled hay-cart, somewhere between an ordinary cart and a trolley

Poss – to wash clothes by putting them in a 'poss-tub' of soap and water and thumping them with a 'poss-stick,' or short-legged staff, in some places called a 'dolly'.

Put – in mining, the 'putter' is a lad who would 'put', or shove the full tubs from the hewer's 'cavil' to the 'flat' and take the empty ones in to him. The empty or 'tume' tub was often called the 'led 'un' (= led one, i.e. the tub led in).

Scoreprice – pitmen's wages, the old price for filling a 'score', i.e. 21 (or, in some places, 25) 'tubs'

Skeel – a peculiarly shaped bucket (broader at bottom than top, with an upright stave projecting from the rim, to serve as a handle), formerly used in colliery villages to carry water for household use. They were carried on women's heads on a 'wase' and a piece of wood was made to float on the top, to prevent the water from splashing over.

Upstanding – regular, fixed, constant (of wages)

The historic marina at Hartlepool iStock

A

Abed – in bed

Abune – above

Ahlnt – behind

Ass – ashes

Ay – yes

B

Bad – poorly, unwell

Baff – the alternate or 'off' day or week ('Baff Saturday', 'Baff week') when the fortnightly wages were not paid to the miners, as opposed to 'Pay Saturday'

Baitpoke – the linen bag in which workmen carried their food

Barley – to claim, to speak for first; as, *'Barley me the big 'un.'*

Berries – generic name for all fruit of the berry kind

Betimes – sometimes; at times

Bit – used adjectivally, as *'a bit garden'* (a little garden), *'a bit lad (or laddie)'*, *'a bit lass (or lassie)'* (a little boy or girl)

Bite – a bit, morsel

Blare – to cry

Bleck – dirty grease, found on coal waggonways where rollers are used

Brock – badger

Bummeler – bumble-bee

A locomotive designed by George Stephenson, a County Durham man and a leading figure in the history of rail. iStock

C

Cage – the lift which goes up and down in a mine shaft

Caller – fresh. The cry of fishwives used to be, *'Caller hair'n (herring)! Fresh, caller hair'n.'* Also a man paid to go round at various hours of the night and early morning, 'calling' miners to get up to go to work, by rapping on their doors. Hence, 'Calling Course', the time a caller goes on his rounds.

Can and could – to be able. *'They'll not can get any food'* – not be able to.

Canny – a north-country catchword. *'A canny few'* = a fair number, a 'canny man' is one with some sense in his head, a *'canny little body'* would be a dapper little person, with some notion of briskness and neatness. *'It'll tak' a canny bit'*, i.e. take some time. Also, careful, gentle. A child is told to be 'canny' with a jug or other fragile article.

Carling Sunday – the Fifth Sunday in Lent, on which day the traditional dish was one of 'carlins' cooked in melted butter. A carling is a kind of pea, of a dark grey or brown colour. They were used by lads on 'Carlin' Sunday' for throwing at one another and were boiled by pub-owners for their customers on that night.

Chinnerly – to separate the larger pieces of coal from the dust

Chuck – food, provisions

Claggum – toffee

Claze or Cleze – clothes

Clever – in good health; well, properly

Clout – a cloth, or old rag

Crack – talk

Cuddy-handed – left-handed

D

Da and Ma – Dad and Mum

Dawd – slice

Deave – to trouble, bother

Delve – to dig

Dene – the picturesque wooded hollows, each crossed by a stream, which line the sea-coast of Durham, are called 'denes'

Doctor – the stickleback, with a black head and reddish belly

Door staingels – door-frames

Dothery – shaky, failing; of old age

Doving – dozing

Duds – clothes

Duff – fine coal, or coal dust. Hence, duffy, trashy, cheap and nasty (of sugar); small (flour or coal); ticklish, hard, awkward.

Dwarmy – faint, languid

Taking a break. The staff of English and Bennett's greengrocer's shop in Chester-le-Street, standing outside their workplace in the 1900s. Durham County Record Office D_CL0027_0277_0036

E

Eneugh – enough
Ettle – to intend, try

F

Fair – to improve, become fair (of weather)
Farntickled – freckled
Fash – to bother
Feck – portion. *'He did the main feck of the work.'*
Femmer – frail
Fetch up – bring up, rear
Fettle (verb and noun) – north-country catchword.
To 'fettle' or 'fettle up', the regular expression for to
'right up', 'get in order', 'repair'; 'in good fettle' (good
condition).
Fiddy faddy – trivial, elaborate, e.g. of fancy work
First – instead of 'next day', the expression was 'day first'
Fley – to scare
Flipe – hat-brim
Flit – to 'shift' or remove from a house by night, unknown
to anybody
Foal foot – coltsfoot, tussilago
Folly tar – a game played with marbles, while walking
along

Fond – foolish; hence 'fondie'; *'Thou's a fondie.'*

Footing, first – the first person who enters one's doors on New Year's Day. This refers to the custom of going round to various houses on the morning of the New Year, soon after the old year has passed, and being greeted by those who humour the custom by keeping open house (bread and cheese, meat and drink, especially the latter) for the first callers.

Forby – besides. *'There was other six forby me.'*

Forebears – ancestors. Sometimes called 'fore-elders'.

Forthless – worthless, useless

Fortnighth – fortnight

Fozy – unsound, of vegetables

Fray – from

Fremd – strange

Fresh – a thaw. *'There's a heavy (or thick) fresh on.'*

Fret – a mist, or sea-fog

G

Gaffer – a 'masterman' or foreman

Gait – way, road. A mining term signifying a short journey.

Gan – go. *'Gan on!'* = *'Now then!' 'Start!'; 'Is thoo gannin'? (Are you going?)*

Gather – make a collection ('gathering') in money

Gee-y – crooked, twisted. *'It's all a-gee-y.'*

Female workers and staff at Birtley Royal Ordnance Factory in 1916.
Durham County Record Office D_DLI0007_1014_0006

Geordie – a miner (compare Jack Tar, Tommy Atkins, 'Johnny' or 'Tommy,' as generic names)

Get off – learn by heart

Gill – a half pint

Gimmers – rascal

Gliff – startle

Glower – to stare with anger or amazement

Gome – to heed

Gowk or gowkie – a soft person

Grape – to grope, search. Also, a kind of shovel (sometimes called 'gripe '), or a huge fork-like implement used in filling coke, and by farmers for removing manure.

Greybird – a song thrush

Guising – play-acting by 'guisers', men and boys in disguise (with blackened faces and paper caps), who went around performing a Christmas play. The play usually went along the following lines:

Characters: The Leader, King George, Doctor Brown, Johnny Funny.

Leader: The moon's gone down, and I've lost my way,
And in this house I mean to stay.
If you don't believe the word I say,
Step in, King George, and clear the way.
(Here comes in King George.)

King George: King George is my name,
A sword and pistol by my side;
I hope I win the game,
The game of the sword.
Let's know your power,
I'll slash you into mincemeat
In less than half an-hour.
Leader: You, sir?
KG: Yes, me, sir!
Leader: Take the sword, and try, sir!
(They fight and the Leader falls.)
KG: Ho, ho! What have I done?
I've killed his father's only son.
Send for the ten-pound doctor.

Johnny Funny: *There's no ten-pound doctor.*
All: *Send for the twenty-pound doctor.*
Dr Brown: *Here comes in old Doctor Brown,*
The best old doctor in the town.
KG: *Who made you the best doctor?*
Dr B: *By my travels.*
KG: *Where did you travel?*
Dr B: *Italy, France, and Spain;*
Three times there, and back again.
KG: *What can you cure?*
Dr B: *A dead man.*
KG: *Cure him.*
Dr B: *I've got a little bottle in my pocket, goes tick-tack.*
Rise up, Jack!
(The Leader rises)
All sing: *My brother's come alive again,*
We'll never fight no more.
We'll be as kind as ever,
As ever we were before,
A pocket full of money,
A cellar full of beer,
I wish you a merry Christmas
And a happy New Year!
The weather's very clarty,
My boots is very thin,
I've got a little money- box,

To put my money in.

(Each then sings a solo.)

Gyoose – goose. *'Like a gyoose cut i' the head,'* i.e. bewildered, 'all abroad'.

A brass band outside Rookhope School in around 1910
Durham County Record Office D_CL0027_0277_0420

H

Ha woy – a call to horses to come to the left or 'near' side

Hack – a heavy pick, weighing about 7Ibs, with a head about 18in in length. There were various kinds, e.g. Tommy hack (round head and chisel point), Jack hack (round head and sharp point), Pick hack (sharp head and chisel point). Also, filth, dirt: *'Aa canna get the hack off tha.'*

Ham – repeat. *'He ham'd it o'er and o'er.'*

Hand's-turn – a stroke of work (common); often, of a 'good turn'

Hant – habit. *'He has a nasty hant of doing that.'*

Happen – this verb was used transitively, e.g. *'he happened it'* (i.e. it happened to him), *'she happened a bad accident.'*

Har away – heard every day and almost every five minutes. *Be off! Come along here!*

Hemmels – originally, a thatched shed, stable, or byre; now the same, though seldom thatched

Hew – to hack away at the coal down a mine. Hence, 'hewer' one who hews coal, a miner.

Hey – a common exclamation of surprise or indifference; *'Hey! Aa din-aa'* (really, I don't know).

Hilly howley – hill and hole. In tossing the bat for innings, 'hill' is the oval side uppermost.

Hind – a farm-labourer.

Hitchy-bay – Hopscotch.

Hogger – hosepipe. Also, the following stocking arrangement: the coal-hewer formerly wore his stockings with the 'feet' cut off, so that when small coals got into the stocking-foot, he had only to pull off this, and not the whole stocking; consequently his ankles were bare, while the stocking-leg covered his calf.

Howdie – midwife.

Howk – to dig or hew out, as, for instance, with a 'hack'.

Hoy – to throw.

Hunkers – haunches. 'Sitting on the hunkers' means squatting, as miners do in the streets (sitting on the toes, with the thighs resting on the calves).

I

Insense – make to understand, 'render sensible', inform
Italian iron – a 'tallion iron was an iron tube about 6in long and pointed at one end. A heater was inserted into the tube. It was used to make the waves in the frills of women's caps.

J

Jowl – to knock on the coal, while working down the mine, so that workmen on the other side knew by the sound how near they were to each other.

Railway station staff, Hesleden in the early 1900s

Durham County Record Office D_CL0027_0277_1942

K

Kail-pot – a crock to boil cabbage (kail)

Keeker – the overlooker on a pit-heap

Kellick – unfledged bird

Ken – knew, known

Kenspreckled – well known, marked

Ket – not good for food

Kibble – a big iron tub, for filling with rubbish, in sinking a shaft

Kit – a small tub for washing in, used by pitmen

Kittle – ticklish, awkward to manage

Kitty – policeman's lock-up. Also, a short straw, about 6in long, filled with powder, and used by miners in firing.

Kitty cat – a game called Tipcat

L

Lad – boy, youth. Also, a common way of addressing horses.

Laid off – discontinued. The invariable description of a pit which is not working is 'laid off' or 'laid in'.

Lang – long

Lap – to wrap

Lay in – to ' lay in' a pit, or lay it idle; to leave off working it, as when it becomes exhausted of coals

Learn – teach

Lignies – quoits made of lignum vitae wood, used in the game '*Spell and Nur*'

Like – likely; 'like to fall'

Limbers – shafts of a carriage. The only name for shafts of a 'tub' down the mine, which are made in one piece and detachable.

Linings – pitmen's drawers, fastened at the knee by strings

Lippen – to depend on, or trust to a person to perform a certain work

Lisk – thigh

List – desire, energy

Loop – to leap, jump

Lops and lice – hips and haws. So called by children.

Low – aflame. Hence 'low-rope' hemp rope steeped in tar, to burn as a torch.

Lowpy-lang-lonnen – leapfrog

Lug – ear

Lum – chimney

M

Make – to *mak' gam'* (make game) of anybody is to make fun of, ridicule, generally in the form '*makkin' gam'*'. To '*mak' sha'p'*, or '*be sharp'* is equivalent to the commoner '*look sharp'*.

Man – as throughout the North, used in exclamations: *'Noo, man!'* = Now, sir. *'Eh, mon, aa din-aa'* = indeed, sir (or mate), I don't know. Also used irrespective of sex.

Marra – mate

Matterless – *'It's matterless'*, an old everyday expression for 'no matter', 'it's immaterial',

Maybe – perhaps

Meat – food. Only used in this wide sense, when speaking of animals' food.

Mense – politeness, kindness. When you invited their friends to dinner as a duty, and they could not come, you were said to *'save your meat and your mense'*. *'It'll be more menseful'* (courteous, hospitable): said of serving up a whole joint, to some guests, rather than the same joint cut up into chops.

Mickle – little

Middenstead – ash-heap

Midgy, also called a Mistress – a kind of lamp used by putters in the mines. The height of the lamp was about 8in, width 3in, with an open front. When first invented, they were simply little wooden boxes, with a hole at the bottom, through which the candle was thrust, and another hole at the top to let out the heat. Afterwards tin took the place of wood. The flame was sheltered by a piece of wood or tin about 2in high from the bottom of the lamp, and a similar piece from the top.

Mind – remember

Moley rat – the mole

Muffler – a neckerchief or 'comforter'

N

Neif – hand

Nevvy – nephew

Nicely – 'How are you?' 'Nicely': a polite expression for *'varry canny'* or *'aa canna com-plee-an'* (complain)

Niffnaffs – nick-nacks

Night – used, as in country parts in the south, of any time after noon

Nimmy – counting-in rhymes recited in starting a round game:

> *Nimmy, nimmy, nak,*
> *Which hand will tha tak'?*
> *The reet or the left,*
> *Or the bonny bord's (bird's) heft?'*

Nor – than

Noration – a confused crowd; a noise

North-countryman – a person from Northumberland or over the Border. *'He cooms fro' the West'* would mean Weardale, Teesdale, or Cumberland. *'Sooth'* (south) would mean anywhere south of the speaker; *'Countryman'* means an agricultural labourer.

Nought – nothing

O

Oftens – often

Oxter – armpit.

Oxter-bound – stiff in arm and shoulder

A summer's day in the high street of the Edwardian town at Beamish Museum in County Durham, England. Beamish is a world-famous open-air museum which portrays past times in North-East England. iStock

P

Peedee – something small, like a tiny marble

Peggin'-top – a peg-top

Pen-point – the nib of a pen

Pen-shank – pen-holder

Perishment – a violent chill was described as a 'perishment of cold'

Pick at – find fault with, abuse

Pipe-stopple – the stem of a tobacco-pipe, sometimes called 'pipe-shank'

Pit – a mine. A miner was always a 'pitman' or 'pittie' and pit dress was 'pit-claes'

Poke – a sack, or bag; 'flour-poke'

Poked – offended

Pollis – police

Pot-pie – a boys' game. All caps are placed on a lad's back, the rest jump over him, 'leapfrog' fashion, and the one who moves a cap becomes vaulting-horse in his turn.

Proggle – a thorn

Puddings – intestines. Hence 'pigs'-puddings', black pudding.

Putting through – a telling off

Q

Quoit – a common game among miners, but also a large white marble made of earthenware, called a 'pot quoit'

R

Rageous – outrageous

Raise – to 'raise the place', to make an uproar

Rame – to ply one with questions

Rank – the distance a 'putter' put the coal from face to flat. The first 'renk' might be 80 yards from the hewer, and as the distance increased, the putter received an additional penny for every 20 yards.

Rasp – raspberry

Rattle-scawp – a playful, mischievous fellow

Rax – stretch

Rear – underdone (of meat)

Reckling – the weak pig in a litter

Reek – smoke; 'baccy- reek', 'powder-reek'

S

Sally Walker – a round game. The players would form a ring, joining hands, and go round a girl in the middle of the ring, singing:

Rise, Sally Walker, rise if you can,
Rise, Sally Walker, to follow your good man.
Choose to the east, choose to the west,
Choose to the bonny lad that you like best.

The girl in the middle would then pick the young man of her choice, and the rest sing

Now ye're married I wish you joy,
First a girl and then a boy.
Seven years over, seven years to come,
Now is your time to kiss and be done.

They would then kiss and go out, to give place to another couple, the game going on as before.

Sark – shirt

Scobb'ie – chaffinch

Second-handed – second-hand

Seggar – soft stone lying on coal-seams, used for making into bricks and coping stones

Siddle – to pick out or choose the best of anything

Slowed – drunk

Slum – slumber

Sneakly – quietly and sly

Spelk – a thorn or splinter (also used of anything insignificant)

Stent – one's fill. *'He's had his stent.'*

Stick and clout – umbrella

Stirk – yearling calf

Stite – equally, as soon. *'Stite him as me'* (the sense was often 'much rather').

Stobbie – unfledged bird

Stour – dust in motion

Strait – narrow

Stramp – trample

T

Tappy-lappy – pell-mell, helter-skelter

Teem – pour. Rain would 'teem in' through a leaking roof. To 'teem out' was to pour out liquids. A teapot with a well-turned spout is called a 'good teemer'.

Tew – to tire, pull about, tease

Tidy betty – a short fender across the grate, without a bottom

Token – a ticket, of tin or leather, attached to each tub of coals, stating details

Troon – a mason's trowel

Tub – a coal waggon used down the pit

Twitch-bell – ear-wig

U

Upgrown – grown up, adult

V

Viewer – the manager of a coal mine. So, 'under-viewer' = under-manager.
Vine – a lead-pencil

W

Waggonway – a colliery line of rails
Warsh – faint, from loss of food
Waysgoose – a day trip for the employees of a firm or company, especially from a newspaper
Whaing – boot-lace
Whiles – once; sometimes
Whin – gorse
Wig – a tea-cake. Same as '*doo*'.
Wiggery waggery – loose motion in walking
Wite – weight; blame
Wor – our *('Oo-ur')*

Y

Yard – common abbreviation for churchyard
Yetling – a small crock
Yoke – Yule
Yon – yonder

Sayings and phrases

Bite the bridle and bear it – Put up with it

I could bite a double tack nail in two – I'm absolutely famished!

We must all stand on our own bottoms or Every tub must stand on its own bottom – We have to stand up for ourselves

I haven't could get across the doors – I've not been able to get out

I doubt I'll not can get – I expect I shan't be able to come

He's not over-clever – He's not very well

Ma canny hinny – A term of endearment

Let's have a bit crack – Let's have a bit of a gossip

Thou's a good crack – You're a good talker!

Not much to crack on – Not enjoying very good health

Eh! aa din-aa – Indeed, I don't know

I haven't been across the doors – I haven't been outdoors

Dear knows – Goodness only knows

Nows and thens – Now and then

Give over – Don't! Stop that!

Well, what fettle? – How are you doing?

By gock – An everyday expression of surprise

As slaa as a horntop – Incredibly slow

The kail-pot's callin' the yetlin' smutty – A common proverb and a local version of the pot calling the kettle black!

Thoo's niver been weshed since the howdie weshed th'
– Sometimes said to a very dirty person!

Soft – wet (of the weather). A common saying on a rainy day is 'Soft!'

He hadn't the scribe of a pen for it – He didn't have a receipt or written guarantee

Out of the way – Used to refer to badly behaved people: 'He's been an out-of-the-way man in his time.'

He's like a nine with the tail cut off – He's a good-for-nothing

My word! – A common exclamation of surprise

Wey ay! – To be sure!

What cheer? – A common greeting, answered back in the same words

Dressed up to the mark – Dressed up to the nines

Looks-tha! – An expression aimed at getting someone's attention

Sitting on the knees – A common way of referring to kneeling: *'He tell'd her to sit upon her knees, so down they sat.'*

How are you keeping? – How are you?

Hupstitch – Every now and again, 'every hupstitch'; e.g. *'He does it every hupstitch.'*

Excerpt from *A list of words and phrases in everyday use by the natives of Hetton-le-Hole in the County of Durham, being words not ordinarily accepted, or but seldom found in the standard English of the day* by Francis Milnes Temple Palgrave, published in 1896.

Coal mining in County Durham

Miners' lodging shops, under construction at Rookhope in the early 1900s. Durham County Record Office D_CL0027_0277_0106

Coal mining has shaped the lives, landscape and language of County Durham in many ways. That's not surprising when you consider that the Durham coalfield extended throughout north, east and central Durham. It is thought that the North-East is the oldest intensive coal mining district in the country. There are even some signs that the Romans excavated coal in County Durham. Local records mention coal as far back as the 12th century. Coal was certainly mined extensively even in the medieval period. In the 1300s, the Lumley mine was owned and run by the monks of Finchale Priory. However it was in the 13th and 14th centuries that coal mining really got going in County Durham. The majority of the early mines were to be found along the River Tyne because the shallow seams were more accessible.

It was during the Industrial Revolution, as you would expect, that the industry became more intensive because of improvements in mining methods and techniques. This would create huge profits for local landowners, including the Bishop of Durham. During this phase, County Durham saw whole communities spring up around the industry and the growth of Pitmatic, the miners' dialect. Coal production in County Durham soared in the mid-1900s, by which time there were no fewer than 170,000 miners working in the area! The mining industry started to decline after the Second World War, leading to the closure of many local pits and the loss of local communities. The last colliery in the Durham coalfield closed in 1994

What is Pitmatic?
Pitmatic is the distinctive name for the dialect spoken in the old mining areas of County Durham and Northumberland. Most of us have heard the saying 'carrying coals to Newcastle' (referring to an unnecessary activity) and, like many sayings, this has its roots in the past, in this instance

referring to the North-East as the capital of mining. It is said that the phrase was first recorded in 1538. Sadly, the last major pit closed in 2005. But for a while, County Durham had a central role in the mining industry.

Coal-hewers at Silksworth in around 1932
Durham County Record Office D_PH0177_0031

The Pitmatic dialect was thought to have been used by people around the Great Northern Coalfield, but more specifically by miners in County Durham in the 1930s.

Previously called *'Pitmatical'* and also nicknamed *'Yakka'*, it features specialised words around pit mining. The dialect is believed to be a wonderful mix of words from Old Norse, Dutch and other languages, as well as some more colourful additions made up by the miners themselves!

The word 'Pitmatic' used to refer to 'the skill of mining'. It is thought to have become more well known when the writer J.B. PRIESTLEY used it when referring to the dialect of East Durham miners following a visit to Durham in 1934:

> *'The local miners have a curious lingo of their own, which they call 'pitmatik'. It is, you might say, a dialect within a dialect, for it is used only by the pitmen when they are talking among themselves. When the pitmen are exchanging stories of colliery life, usually very grim stories, they do it in 'pitmatik', which is Scandinavian in origin.'*

The mysteries of Pitmatic even ended up confusing supporters of the miners when they wanted to speak to them in order to help improve their working conditions in the 1840s! The County Durham comedian BOBBY THOMPSON was well known for using Pitmatic in his act. These days, if you head to some areas of the coast of Northumberland and listen carefully, you may still hear Pitmatic spoken by the locals.

Pitmatic glossary

Bait – a packed meal

Baitpoke – a bag to carry the meal in

Blogged up – when a pipe became blocked up with dirt

Brat – an inferior type of coal

Canch – the stone below the floor of a narrow coal seam that has to be removed as coal-getting proceeds

Clag – to stick

Clarts – mud

Dab-hand – a capable or efficient worker

Dataller – also known as a day-man, was given work on an ad hoc, daily basis

Deputy – the man in charge of the safety of the men underground

Dollyshutting – blasting down coal without undercutting

Fettle – to repair or mend

For-fairs – no sneaky or underhand work

Fullick – a blow of great force

Graithe – to make ready or repair

Grove – a gap in a seam from which coal has been taken

Hacky – dirty or filthy

Hewer – a coal miner, a person who cut the coal

Hoggers – the shorts that miners wore in the pit

Howk – to dig or scoup out, or punish

Keeker – the surface foreman responsible for the coal

Ket – filth or rubbish

Mell – a large wood or iron hammer

Met – a measurement marked on a stick

Midgey – an open-fronted flame lantern

Powder-reek – smoke caused by firing a shot in the pit

Rammel – the stone that gets mixed with the coal in the pit

Rive – to tear

Rolley – a waggon for transporting coal

Rolleyway – a pathway high enough for a horse to pass

Scapipen – a way of getting coal without blasting

Shaftsinker – the person employed to sink the shafts of a new mine

Shotfirer – the person who lays charges and carries out the explosions to bring down the coal

Skeets – guides for the cages in the pit shaft

Smart-money – compensation

Stythe – bad air

Swalley – a dip or hollow on a roadway

Tommy hack – a combined hammer and chisel ended pick used by rolleywaymen

Trapper – a child who opened and closed the door in the roadway through which coal was brought

Wedger – anything particularly large

Whimsey – a turntable from which a rope is uncoiled

Winder – the person responsible for the winding engine which raised and lowered the cage that brought the coal and the men out of the pit

A view of coal mining in the past

Life was tough as a coal miner, as we can see from this account of the industry in County Durham, written in the late 1800s:

To its mining industry Durham is chiefly indebted for the high rank which it holds amongst the English counties, the benefit derived being estimated, not according to the direct marketable value of the minerals, but by their influence in developing the manufacturing power of the country. With regard to the coal trade, it can scarcely be necessary for us to point out to the reader its vast importance. Deprive us of our coal and where would be our manufactures? No longer should we, by our commerce, convey the conjoining benefits of knowledge and civilisation to the remote regions of the earth. No longer should we triumph over time and space, no longer traverse the land with a rapidity which has exceeded all anticipation, nor the ocean with a swiftness and certainty which brings the far east within the voyage of a few days. The period at which coal was first wrought in the north is not known with any degree of certainty, but we find it noticed in record by the charter of Henry III, in 1215, which granted permission to mine it. It seems to have been known in the fourteenth century, not only in London, but also in France, though it did not become an article of commerce till the latter part of the sixteenth century.

First, then, how to descend. We see a vertical hole, or pit, pitchy dark, and surmounted by wheels to facilitate the raising of coal from the bottom of the shaft. Into one of the ' tubs', or ' buckets', used for this purpose, we must now contrive to get, a matter which requires no small amount of nerve to effect. If the bottom of the bucket should give way, or the rope break, or – but it is fearful to speculate on such ifs, when you are swinging over a depth of several hundred feet Now we are descending. It is said by those who ascend in balloons, that no feeling of motion is perceptible, but that the earth seems to be flying away from them, while they are perfectly still and motionless. Much the same idea may be said, in reverse, in descending a coal shaft. You have no idea of the descent, but the little round hole of light seems to be flying faster and faster over your head upwards, as if it were going to the skies, and at length, in a couple of minutes, perhaps – the orifice of the shaft has apparently turned itself into a day-star, which shines far, far above you in the firmament.

THE WORKING AND MANAGEMENT DISCIPLINE AND DUTIES OF A COAL MINE

The persons engaged in a colliery are sub-divided into a greater number of classes than might, perhaps, be supposed, and, generally speaking, the technical designations of these classes are more significant than is usually observable in other industrial occupations, but some of these sound strangely enough to the ears of the uninitiated. They are distinguished into the two groups of underground and upperground establishments, the former engaged in the pit, and the latter in conducting the open-air arrangements. The chief of them are occupied in a way which may be illustrated in the following connected view.

The actual coal digger is called the hewer. Whether the seam be so narrow that be can hardly creep into it on his hands and knees, or whether it be lofty enough for him to stand upright in, he is the responsible workman who loosens the coal from its bed; all the arrangements below ground are made to suit him; he is indeed the key of the pit, the centre of the mining system.

The hewers are like the cabinet council of the country, governing and directing and working for the whole pit population besides. Next to them come the putters, who are divided into train headsmen, foals, and half-marrows. These are all youths or children, and their employment consists in dragging or pushing the coals from the workings to the passages where horses are capable of being employed in the work. The distance that a corve, or basket of coal, is dragged in this manner, averages about a hundred and fifty yards. When a boy 'puts' or drags a load by himself he is designated a tram, when two boys of unequal age and strength assist each other, the elder is called a headsman and the younger a foal, and when two boys of equal age and strength help each other, both are styled half-marrows. When the corves are 'put' to a particular place, where a crane is fixed, the crane-man manages the crane by which the corves are transferred from the tramway to the rolleys, and keeps an account of the number so transferred. The corf is a wicker-work basket, containing from four to seven hundred weights, the rolley is a waggon for transporting the corves from the crane to the shaft, and the rolleyway is a road, or path, sufficiently high for a horse to walk along it and is kept in repair by the rolleyway-men, The driver takes charge of the horse, which draws the rolley, and the on-setter is stationed at the bottom of the shaft, to hook and unhook the corves and tubs which have descended or are about to ascend the shaft.

In addition to the varieties of pitmen which we have mentioned, there are numerous others, such as furnacemen, horse-keepers, lamp-keepers, shifters, switch-keepers, trappers, way -cleaners, and water leaders. Many of these strange designations find a place in the popular songs and stories of the colliery district – songs and stories which are like an unknown tongue to the stranger, until he acquires a knowledge of the vocabulary in which they are composed.

From the enumeration of the officers and men given above, the reader will plainly perceive, that colliers are not merely black-faced diggers and shovellers, who attack the coal wherever they meet with it, and roam about in a dark pit to seek their coaly fortunes. All is pre-arranged and systematic; every one knows exactly whither he is to go, and what he has to do. But the preceding list, formidable as it appears, does by no means include all those engaged at a colliery – they are nearly all of them the "underground' hands, who could not transmit the coal to the market without the aid of the 'upperground' establishment, which comprises barksmen, brakesmen, waiters, trimmers, staith-men, screen-trappers, and many others.

Excerpt from *History, Topography, and Directory of the County Palatine of Durham*, by WILLIAM WHELLAN & Co., published in 1856

Women and children pick coal at Esh Winning Colliery village in the 1950s Durham County Record Office D_CL0027_0277_1750

The Collier's Rant

The tradition of capturing the experiences of County Durham's miners goes back many years. Just one example of this is a poem about the experience of a collier, part of the collection The Northumberland Garland by Joseph Ritson, published in 1809. In it, you can find examples of local dialect words, like 'marrow', which means 'mate' or 'friend'.

As me and my marrow was ganning to wark,
We met with the devil, it was in the dark;
I up with my pick, it being in the neit,
I knock'd off his horns, likewise his club feet.

Follow the horses, Johnny my lad oh!
Follow them through, my canny lad oh!
Follow the horses, Johnny my lad oh!
O lad ly away, canny lad oh!

As me and my marrow was putting the tram.
The low it went out, and my marrow went wrang.
You would have laugh'd had you seen the gam.
The deil gat my marrow, but I gat the tram.

Follow the horses, &c.

Oh! marrow, oh! marrow, what dost thou think?
I've broken my bottle, and spilt a' my drink;
I lost a' my shin -splints among the great stanes,
Draw me t' the shaft, it's time to gane hame.

Follow the horses, &c.

Oh! marrow, oh! marrow, where hast thou been?
Driving the drift from the low seam,
Driving the drift, &c.
Had up the low, lad, deil stop out thy een!

Follow the horses, &c.

Oh! marrow, oh! marrow, this is wor pay week.
We'll get penny loaves and drink to wor beek;
And we'll fill up our bumper, and round it shall go.
Follow the horses, Johnny lad oh!

Follow the horses, &c.

There is my horse, and there is my tram;
Twee horns full of grease will make her to gang!
There is my hoggers, likewise my half shoon,
And smash my heart, marrow, my putting's a' done.

> *Follow the horses, Johnny my lad oh!*
> *Follow them through, my canny lad oh!*
> *Follow the horses, Johnny my lad oh!*
> *Oh! lad ly away, canny lad oh*

Excerpt from *Northern Garlands*, a collection of songs by JOSEPH RITSON, published in 1809

Escomb Church in Bishop Auckland, one of the oldest Anglo-Saxon churches in England, as it looked in the 1920s
Durham County Record Office D_PH0258_0033

The 'Pitman Poets' of County Durham

Tommy Armstrong

Known affectionately as *'The Pitman Poet'*, TOMMY ARMSTRONG was born in 1848 in Shotley Bridge, County Durham. Tommy was to become one of the best-loved poetic voices of both his mining community and the wider public. He captured the experiences of the mining people so powerfully that his works are well loved to this day.

As you would expect for a figure known as *'The Pitman Poet'* or *'The Bard of the Northern Coalfield'*, Tommy worked for most of his life in the collieries at Addison, East Tanfield, Tanfield Moor and Tanfield Lea. However, there was also a phase when he lived and worked in Whitley Bay as a newsagent! Tommy had had rickets as a child and suffered from a lifelong leg disability as a result. It was because of this that he had to be carried to work when he was young. His song *The South Medomsley Strike* has been described as the greatest mining song ever written.

While a few of his songs were on the lighter side, the majority of them reflected the challenging and dangerous work conditions endured by the miners. Tommy's most famous songs are *Dorham Jail*, *Wor Nanny's A Maisor* and *Trimdon Grange Explosion*. The first of these was inspired by a brief spell in Durham jail, as a result of Tommy's enjoyment of the drink.

Ye'l awl hev ard o' Dorham
But it wad ye much sorprise
To see the prisoners in the yard,
When they're on exorcise
The yard is built eroond wi' walls,
Se' noabil and se' strang,
Whe ivor gans there heh te bide
Thor time be it short or lang

CHORUS
There's nee gud luck in Dorham Jail
Theres nee gud luck at awl
Whats the breed en skilly for
But just te make ye small

Tommy became relied upon to record the real-life events affecting his fellow miners. One of the most famous examples of this was his song, *Trimdon Grange Explosion*, which captured the horror of an explosion that caused the death of seventy-four men and boys in 1882. The song was intended to raise money in aid of the families affected by the disaster. Because he realised that this poem would be heard by an audience wider than the mining community, Tommy wrote it in standard English rather than in dialect.

Tommy's own words from his poem *The Durham Strike* are engraved on his headstone:

> *The miners of Northumberland we shall for ever praise,*
> *For being so kind in helping us those tyrannising days;*
> *We thank the other counties too, that have been doing the same*
> *For every man who reads will know that we are not to blame.*

Jock Purdon

GEORGE 'JOCK' PURDON, as you can probably guess from his nickname, was originally from Scotland and was born in 1925. However, it was his move to County Durham and his life as a pit miner in Chester-le-Street which led to Purdon's standing as a British poet and songwriter and an important voice of the mining people. He soon became known as 'the miner's poet'.

A twist of fate meant that Purdon was conscripted as a miner during World War II, due to the labour shortage. He settled in Chester-le-Street after the war and continued to work in the pits. It is this experience which led to the publication of his book, *Songs of the Durham Coalfield*. This featured songs such as *The Easington Explosion*, an account of a terrible accident in which eighty-one miners perished. Purdon is also recognised for coining the word *Pitracide*, which meant to 'to murder a pit for economic reasons'. But there's humour among the tales of hardship. The song *Hally's Piebald Gallowa* recalls the sad loss of the Lumley pit banner, which was eaten by a Galloway pony, one of the animals used to take coal carts underground!

Purdon's lifelong commitment to his mining community motivated him to perform for the benefit of striking miners in the 1984–85 miners' strike. He also appeared at the Royal Albert Hall in the *'Concert for Heroes'* in 1985.

Nicknames from the North-East

The North-East has some distinctive names for its local people. Here's a quick guide to help you get your references right!

'Geordies'

The term 'Geordie' is arguably the best-known name for people from up North. This is generally a name for people who hail from Tyneside. However, there is a little bit of an overlap in terms of areas, because the name is also linked with some Northern parts of County Durham. As well as being a nickname for the locals, Geordie also serves as the name of the local dialect. Like the next nickname we'll look at, this moniker is thought to come from the North-East coal mines, although this has not been conclusively proven and there are various counter-arguments. Geordie is also sometimes called Tyneside English.

'Pit Yakkers'

Residents of County Durham are still sometimes known as Pit Yakkers. This is because the local mining dialect, as we saw earlier in this book, was known in the area as Pitmatic or Yakka. The nickname Pit Yakker was originally given to miners and other residents of the pit villages in the North-East. The other association is that the word 'yakker' was thought to have been the local word for 'hewer', a man who worked at the coalface.

Two women at Pelton Fell, with their canine companion in around 1910.
Durham County Record Office
D_CL0027_0277_0258

'Mackems'

While Sunderland locals may have once called themselves Geordies, they now have their own distinctive nickname: Mackem. The spelling of the name varies, but the name is thought to be based on the local lingo for 'Make Them' ('Mak' 'em'). Again, this nickname is also the name for their local dialect. As with many of the local nicknames there is a football association, as Mackem is also a name for a fan of Sunderland AFC. But the history of this nickname is debatable. Some theories take its pedigree back quite a few years, while others argue that it is a very recent invention.

'Smoggies'

This quirky nickname is a more recent invention. The longer version is Smogmonster and refers to a person from Teesside, specifically Middlesbrough and Stockton. It is thought that this nickname is a reference to the 'smog' produced by the industrial plants based on the River Tees. The name Smoggie is said to be derived from a not very nice way of referring to supporters of Middlesbrough FC as created by fans of Sunderland AFC! However, it's good to see that this once negative association has now disappeared, with Smoggies themselves taking on the nickname with pride.

A Dickensian connection

County Durham has an important connection with the great Victorian author, CHARLES DICKENS. Dickens stayed at Barnard Castle while he was in the process of gathering material for one of his greatest works and third novel, *Nicholas Nickleby*. WILLIAM SHAW's Academy in Bowes (which is now a private home) was the model for Dotheboys Hall in *Nicholas Nickleby*. The character of WACKFORD SQUEERS was said to be inspired by Shaw, who was the headmaster of Bowes Academy in the 1830s. The author's purpose in writing about this was to expose the reality of life in what were then known as 'Yorkshire schools'. These were schools in different parts of the country (not just Yorkshire, despite the name) where people would send unwanted children. They were not nice places. Dickens was also moved by the fate of a boy, GEORGE ASHTON TAYLOR, whose graveside he visited in Bowes. This experience inspired him to create the poignant character of SMIKE in *Nicholas Nickleby*.

Bowes Museum, Barnard Castle in 1892
Durham County Record Office D_CL0005_0037

Cutting the mustard

If you enjoy a dash of English mustard with your meals, you may be interested to know that the city of Durham is the birthplace of your favourite condiment! The creation of modern English mustard was sparked by the inventiveness of a woman called MRS CLEMENTS, who ran a mill in Sadler Street in Durham. While she jealously guarded the details of her new method, we do know that the process involved grinding mustard seeds like flour. This approach was so effective that it soon earned the approval of no less august a figure than KING GEORGE I. It was later on that the business was sold to the Colmans of Norwich.

Mrs Clements' invention helped to generate other industries in the area. One of these was a pottery in Gateshead which was dedicated to supplying pots for the export of, yes, you guessed it, mustard! It was for these reasons that Durham was once synonymous with mustard. The association was even immortalised in local slang that referred to 'knock-kneed Durham men' due to the way they ground mustard seeds between their knees! Mustard production no longer goes on in Durham, although you can still purchase a jar of mustard bearing Mrs Clements' name from the East India Company.

Serious history

Together, Durham Cathedral and Durham Castle make up one of the first sites to be made a UNESCO World Heritage Site. It's no wonder when you consider that both buildings are significant monuments of the Norman Conquest and packed with political history.

Seeking Sanctuary at Durham Cathedral

The Sanctuary Knocker on the North Door of Durham Cathedral is famous for its fascinating history of offering a place of safety to those accused of serious crimes. The tradition was that any person who 'had committed a great

offence' could use the cathedral knocker for 37 days of
sanctuary. They could use that time to make peace with
their enemies or to find a way of leaving England for good.
The entrance to the cathedral originally had two small
chambers above the door. This chamber had windows
through which monks would watch for sanctuary-seekers, so
they could be let in immediately, whatever the time of day
or night. When a sanctuary-seeker arrived, the Galilee bell
would be rung. The person would then be given a black robe
to wear. This had St Cuthbert's Cross on the left shoulder
to show the person had been granted sanctuary by God and

Durham Cathedral iStock

his saint. In the Middle Ages, all churches had a limited right of sanctuary. This simply meant that a person could find shelter and be safe from pursuit for a short period of attack. But only a small number of churches and cathedrals could provide an extended level of sanctuary against the most serious crimes. The Sanctuary Knocker you will see today at Durham Cathedral is a replica of the 12th-century original.

iStock

The world's oldest railway bridge Durham County Record Office D_CL0027_0277_1626

The world's oldest railway bridge

County Durham is the home of Causey Arch, the world's oldest surviving single-arch railway bridge. To be found to this day near Stanley, the bridge was built back in 1725. At that time, it was the longest single-span bridge in the country, covering an impressive 31 metres. But here's something even more impressive about the Causey Arch ... it was built by one man! It's nice to think that stonemason RALPH WOOD would be incredibly proud if he knew that his creation was still standing today!

The birthplace of the railway

County Durham has many reasons to be proud of its past. Yet another one is that it is considered to be the birthplace of the railway. This is because the world's first public railway, between Stockton and Darlington, came into being in 1825 when *Locomotion No.1* was built by GEORGE STEPHENSON.

iStock

In fact, railways, or waggonways, went even further back than this, thanks to the close link between transport from horse-drawn carriages and coal. Horse-drawn carriages were used for pulling coal out of the mines and taking it to the river boats on the Tyne from the 17th century. A network of lines linked collieries on both sides of the Tyne to the river. The waggonways used horses hauling waggons on wooden wheels on wooden rails. Waggonways became so closely linked with Tyneside that they were known throughout the rest of Britain as 'Tyneside Roads'. While it was not a commercial success, it did have a direct connection with the development of what would one day be a fully functional network of railway lines.

It was the Tanfield Railway (or waggonway as it was known at the time) which really put County Durham on the map. This was because it was a great engineering achievement. Tanfield Railway is said to be the world's oldest railway and will be the first railway to celebrate its tricentenary, in 2025!

Wylam's place in rail history

We have the village of Wylam to thank for the modern railway. One of the children who attended the local village school was WILLIAM HEDLEY, who designed *Puffing Billy*, the locomotive which helped to shape the future of rail. Did they put something in the water at Wylam? Later on, it was the birthplace of TIMOTHY HACKWORTH and GEORGE STEPHENSON, two central figures in the development of railways!

Stephenson was very much influenced by *Puffing Billy*. His gauge is still used to this day on the rail network, while his other invention, *Locomotion No. 1* (on which he collaborated with Hackworth) was the template for steam locomotives for many years.

The Puffing Billy steam train iStock

A comic connection

iStock

LAUREL AND HARDY are icons of comedy. But did you know that one half of this entertaining twosome hails from County Durham? Stan Laurel was baptised and educated in Bishop Auckland, having moved away from his birthplace of Cumbria as a child. A statue of the popular comic now stands in the town. You can find it on the site of the Eden Theatre where Laurel's father once worked.

Elizabeth Barrett Browning

The famous poet ELIZABETH BARRETT BROWNING was born in Coxhoe Hall in the village of Coxhoe, County Durham in 1806. One of the most popular writers of her age, her poetry was loved in England and the United States during her lifetime and remains popular to this day.

iStock

The most famous lamp post in the world?

Did you know that the city of Durham is believed by many to be the location of the most famous lamp post in literature? That's because the author of the much-loved children's book, *The Lion, the Witch and the Wardrobe*, C.S. LEWIS, lectured at Durham for a brief period.

It is thought that he noticed one particular lamp post in a picturesque setting in Durham and it is this which inspired the captivating image of the lamp post in the fictional world of Narnia!

The inspiration behind Alice in Wonderland

Alice in Wonderland is a firm favourite of both adults and children alike. It is said to owe much of its extraordinary character to the memories treasured by its author, CHARLES DODGSON (better known as LEWIS CARROLL), of his childhood in the rectory at Croft-on-Tees. Croft Rectory is privately owned, but visitors can visit Croft Church and search out the carving of a grinning cat on a stone seat which is believed to have inspired the creation of the CHESHIRE CAT in *Alice in Wonderland*.

The Cheshire Cat Public Domain

An antiquary from County Durham

Who would have thought that an aficionado of antiques born in County Durham in 1752 in would still be influencing culture to this day? JOSEPH RITSON was born in Stockton-on-Tees. Alongside his career as a conveyancer, he had many extra-curricular passions, including literature and antiques. Never afraid of speaking (or writing) his mind, Ritson made public statements about the quality of people's writing and editing which caused outrage in the educated classes of his day. He was undaunted by the mighty figures of SAMUEL JOHNSON and GEORGE STEEVENS and made negative comments about their version of Shakespeare.

But at least he worked to the same standards he enforced on others, being utterly dedicated to ensuring that the content of the ballads and songs he collected and edited was as accurate as possible. One of these great works was his collection of ballads about Robin Hood. It is thought that this has helped to shape how we see Robin Hood to this day. Sadly, Ritson only grew more eccentric as time went on. One sign of this was that he started using his own system of spelling in his books. Sadly for a County Durham man who helped to capture so many songs and stories for posterity, Ritson ended up going insane.

Why was County Durham known as the County Palatine of Durham?

County Durham was once known as 'the County Palatine of Durham' or 'Bishopric of Durham'. On the surface of it, the reason for this seems fairly straightforward: the County Palatine of Durham was an area in the North of England controlled by the Bishops of Durham. But this county has been known for a long time as County Durham, making it unique in the sense that it is the only English county name to have to be preceded by the word County.

The reason for this goes all the way back to the Bishops of Durham. For many years, they ruled Durham as a county palatine. Which brings us to another question: what was a county palatine or palatinate? Simply put, it was a place which was ruled by a nobleman who was lucky enough have complete autonomy from the rest of the empire. While the nobleman of course had to show that he was loyal to the king, he was free to rule without the king interfering! It was thanks to the Normans that this system was created in the first place. But the whole area had actually been known as the Liberty of Durham and it was under the control of the Bishop of Durham. So that meant that it also went by the catchy names of the *'Liberty of St Cuthbert's Land'*, *'The lands of St Cuthbert between Tyne and Tees'* or even *'The Liberty of Haliwerfolc'!*

Durham in the 19th century iStock

This special power was based on claims which went back a very long way. In essence, it meant that the Lord Bishop of Durham was seen as a second king in England! All this makes County Durham a special place. For many years, it was an independent state ruled by Prince Bishops rather than the king. In fact, the bishops were so powerful that they were able to do everything from running their own armies to raising taxes to making revenue from mines to minting their own coins! These powers were limited to the part of Northumbria which lay south of the rivers Tyne and Derwent and it was this area which grew to be known as the 'County Palatine of Durham' and which is known to this day as County Durham – 'The Land of the Prince Bishops'.

Clog dancing

Toe-tapping miners? That's right and it's all thanks to the tradition of clog dancing which swept through County Durham and other parts of the country! While it might seem surprising to connect miners with clog dancing, the activity was viewed as a sport and associated with boxing contests.

Clog dancing is thought to have started in England as far back as the 1400s as a way of creating entertainment – and keeping warm! For Victorian workers in the Lancashire cotton mills, clogs were an affordable form of footwear, as well as being comfortable for wearing in the cotton mills. While sitting at their weaving machines wearing their hard-soled shoes, the workers would tap their feet to the rhythms of the machines to keep them warm. They would hold dancing competitions during their breaks and lunches and their performances would be judged on the best rhythm patterns.

Three miners, believed to be from the Consett area in about 1930 Durham Durham County Record Office D_CL0027_0277_0015

The main participants in this activity were the male workers. While the wooden clogs were replaced by leather shoes and wooden soles, this then changed to shoes in which two wooden pieces made up the heel and toe. The older form of clogging was thought to be simpler than its later form. In later years, clog dancing became very serious, with big competitions in which the dancers would compete in music halls. This could earn the entrants a championship belt or even a big cash prize! The participants danced to hornpipe tunes and the rules were strict: no upper body movement, arms held by the side, marks for timing, execution and originality. They even danced on pedestals, where of course the most important rule was not to fall off!

The craze for clog dancing had started to decline by the early 20th century. Fortunately, people started to recognise the importance of clog dancing and to this day you can still find clog dancers in different parts of the country, including County Durham.

The Rapper Dance

Yet another form of musical movement has links with the collieries of County Durham. Rapper sword (also known as the 'Short Sword' dance) is a traditional sword dance which first developed among the miners of County Durham and Northumberland. In the dance, five performers move around each other to traditional folk music while using swords made from flexible steel. We're back to interesting footwear again, as with clog dancing, because the dancers wore special shoes that allowed them to make foot movements and create a sound. While this eye-catching ritual came into its own in the 18th and 19th centuries, it is believed that the tradition goes back to an older dance performed by miners in the 1700s. Like clog dancing, the rapper dance started dying out, but was saved by fans and is still performed to this day.

The Lambton Worm

The Lambton Worm is a popular song around the Tyneside area. It recounts an old legend from County Durham and is set around the River Wear in the town of Lambton and at Penshaw Hill, between Durham and Sunderland. The Lambton Worm is based on a legend dating back to medieval times about a giant worm which was the terror of the region!

The old English form of the word worm (or wyrm) refers to a huge snake or dragon. Though slightly different versions of the tale are told all around the area, it is one of the North-East's most famous pieces of folklore, having been adapted from written and oral tradition into pantomime and song formats. The story is essentially the tale of a man and a huge snake and involves battles, karma and a long-standing family curse! The hero of the tale is a young man called John Lambton, who is the heir of the Lambton estate in County Durham. It is on a fishing trip that he reels in a curious catch which he decides to throw down a well instead of returning it to the river. The decision comes back to haunt John, but it all ends well eventually – apart from the family curse!

One interpretation of The Lambton Worm is that it refers to taxation, specifically a tax that the real-life Lord Lambton first invented, then dramatically reduced because of the economic hardship it was causing. The song features a major local landmark still standing today: the Penshaw Monument, which stands on Penshaw Hill. In some variations of the story, it is this hill that the worm curls itself around. The worm is large enough to be able to wind itself around the hill three times, or even nine or ten times in some versions! However, some locals that believe the hill in the story is actually the nearby Worm Hill. Try reading or even singing The Lambton Worm in a traditional North-East accent!

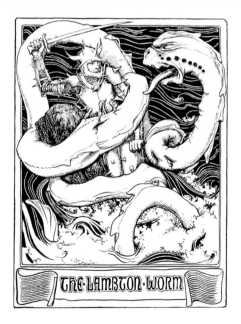

THE·LAMBTON·WORM

The Lambton Worm

One Sunday morn young Lambton went
A-fishin' in the Wear;
An' catched a fish upon he's heuk,
He thowt leuk't varry queer.
But whatt'n a kind of fish it was
Young Lambton cuddent tell.
He waddn't fash te carry'd hyem,
So he hoyed it doon a well.
Chorus: Whisht! Lads, haad yor gobs,
An Aa'll tell ye's aall an aaful story
Whisht! Lads, haad yor gobs,
An' Aa'll tell ye 'boot the worm.
Noo Lambton felt inclined te gan
An' fight i' foreign wars.
he joined a troop o' Knights that cared
For nowther woonds nor scars,
An' off he went te Palestine
Where queer things him befel,
An' varry seun forgat aboot
The queer worm i' the well.
But the worm got fat an' growed and' growed
An' growed an aaful size;
He'd greet big teeth, a greet big gob,
An' greet big goggle eyes.
An' when at neets he craaled aboot
Te pick up bits o' news,
If he felt dry upon the road,
He milked a dozen coos.
This feorful worm wad often feed

On caalves an' lambs an' sheep,
An' swally little bairns alive
When they laid doon te sleep.
An' when he'd eaten aall he cud
An' he had had he's fill,
He craaled away an' lapped he's tail
Seven times roond Pensher Hill.
The news of this myest aaful worm
An' his queer gannins on
Seun crossed the seas, gat te the ears
Ov brave and' bowld Sor John.
So hyem he cam an' catched the beast
An' cut 'im in twe haalves,
An' that seun stopped he's eatin' bairns,
An' sheep an' lambs and caalves.
So noo ye knaa hoo aall the foaks
On byeth sides ov the Wear
Lost lots o' sheep an' lots o' sleep
An' leeved i' mortal feor.
So let's hev one te brave Sor John
That kept the bairns frae harm,
Saved coos an' caalves by myekin' haalves
O' the famis Lambton Worm.
Final Chorus
Noo lads, Aa'll haad me gob,
That's aall Aa knaa aboot the story
Ov Sor John's clivvor job
Wi' the aaful Lambton Worm.

Sources and further reading

www.tanfield-railway.co.uk/history.php

www.houghtonlespring.org.uk/articles/pitmatic_guide_book.pdf

www.thenorthernecho.co.uk/history/1672898.Modern_English_mustard_had_its_roots_in_the_inventiveness_and_energy_of_a_Durham_woman/

www.information-britain.co.uk/countydidyouknow.php?county=32

www.historic-uk.com/HistoryUK/HistoryofBritain/Steam-trains-railways/

www.independent.co.uk/news/science/one-of-the-great-inventions-that-never-was-ndash-until-now-2096805.html

www.telegraph.co.uk/finance/property/advice/
propertymarket/3301903/Desolate-dale-that-took-a-
poets-fancy.html

www.indigogroup.co.uk/durhamdialect/

www.englandsnortheast.co.uk/CoalMiningandRailways.html

www.telegraph.co.uk/culture/books/bookreviews/5893189/
From-Alices-Wonderland-to-a-Roman-Wonderwall-feature.
html

www.durhamrecordoffice.org.uk/Pages/
CoalminingandDurhamcollieries.aspx

www.telegraph.co.uk/travel/destinations/europe/
uk/8796498/Durham-and-the-legacy-left-by-King-Coal.html

Available now from Bradwell Books

Black Country Dialect

Bristol Dialect

Buckinghamshire Dialect

Cockney Dialect

Cornish Dialect

County Durham Dialect

Derbyshire Dialect

Devon Dialect

Dorset Dialect

Essex Dialect

Evolving English WordBank

Glaswegian Dialect

Gloucestershire Dialect

Hampshire Dialect

Kent Dialect

Lancashire Dialect

Leicestershire Dialect

Lincolnshire Dialect

Liverpool Dialect

Manchester Dialect

Newcastle upon Tyne Dialect

Norfolk Dialect

Nottinghamshire Dialect

Scottish Dialects

Somerset Dialect

Suffolk Dialect

Sussex Dialect

The Lake District Dialect

Warwickshire Dialect

Welsh English Dialect

Wiltshire Dialect

Yorkshire Dialect

See website for more details: bradwellbooks.com